A CHANGE IN THE CLIMATE

Also by Edward Storey

Poetry

North Bank Night
A Man in Winter
The Dark Music
A Slant of Light
Last Train to Ely

Prose

Portrait of the Fen Country
Four Seasons in Three Countries
The Solitary Landscape
Call it a Summer Country
Spirit of the Fens
Fen, Fire & Flood
The Winter Fens
Fen Country Christmas
In Fen-country Heaven
Letters from the Fens

Biography

A Right to Song: A Life of John Clare

Autobiography

Fen Boy First

Libretti

Katharine of Aragon (music by Barry Ferguson)
Old Scarlett (music by Trevor Hold)
No Cross, No Crown (music by David Twigg)
The Journey (music by David Twigg)

Edward Storey

A Change in the Climate

Rockingham Press

Published in 1998
by
The Rockingham Press
11 Musley Lane,
Ware, Herts
SG12 7EN

British Library Cataloguing-in-Publication Data

A catalogue record for this book
is available from the British Library

ISBN 1 873468 59 8

Printed in Great Britain
by Biddles Limited, Guildford

Printed on Recycled Paper

Eastern Arts
Board Funded

For Angela

When earth breaks up and heaven expands,
How will the change strike me and you
In the house not made with hands?

Robert Browning

Acknowledgments

Several of these poems first appeared in the following magazines – *Acumen; The Interpreter's House; The Month; Outposts; The Spectator* and *Ver Poets* anthologies.

'Foldings' has been borrowed from my autobiography *Fen Boy First* because it helped to complete the sequence of family poems in this collection. My thanks are due to Robert Hale Ltd.

Contents

LIFE-STORY   9
THE PUMP   11
THE SHED   13
YELLOW FLAG-IRISES   15
FORBIDDEN FLOWERS   16
FOLDINGS   17
THE PIANO   18
THE WIRELESS AERIAL   20
INCIDENTAL MUSIC   22
BRICKYARD WORKERS AT DAYBREAK   23
BUTTER-FINGERS   24
FATHER'S WEDDING-RING   25
DEATH OF AN UNCLE   26
FAILING SIGHT   27
WHITER THAN THE SNOW   28
NEW YEAR'S EVE – 1997   29
TRACING MY FINGER NOW
        ON SIDEBOARD, CHAIRS   31
THE DESTROYER   32
CARROTS   33
COME-UPPANCE   34
THAT PLACE, THOSE HOURS   35
A CHANGE IN THE CLIMATE   36
THE INHERITOR   37
ASKING AGAIN   39
SUNDAY AFTERNOON IN A FENLAND CEMETERY   40
A CHANGE OF VIEW   42
AND WHAT IS SUMMER STILL   43
FEELING EARTH PAUSE   45
CAUGHT ON A MORNING   46

IN AN ALIEN HEAVEN 47
HERON 48
BIRDS IN MOURNING 49
THE SUNFLOWER 50
WAR-CEMETERY – POLAND 51
SURVIVOR 52
THE FACE 53
YOU ASK ME WHAT I'M GOING TO PUT ON 55
EVENING LIGHT 57
LOST DAYS 58
END OF TERM 59
A GIRL WRITING 60
MONUMENTS 61
BEETHOVEN'S STATUE 62
BEETHOVEN 63
SCHUBERT 65
GOOD FRIDAY – SPAIN 66
THE BEES OF ST GUTHLAC 67
SOMETHING OF A GAMBLE 69
AN OLD POET READING TO A YOUNG AUDIENCE 70
THE UNWANTED SOLITUDE 71
EXPERIENCE 72

LIFE-STORY

Daybreak: and I see you rising for work,
rummaging through the last shadows of sleep
before creeping downstairs and into the street
on your way to the farm.   The first one up,
the last to bed.   Each mile from the town
the only chance you'd have to yourself,
to dream it might have been different once.
Not much of a life for a girl who came
from nobody's love and in need of a home.

Little you knew of what could have been yours –
the first flirtation, the carefree dance;
your childhood was over before you grasped
the joys and burdens of innocence.
I stare at your picture in black and white,
wide-eyed and fresh yet tense with a frown
that betrays the presence of pain unborn;
a daughter caught in a world of her own
when death broke more than the dark earth's crust.

Then courtship and vows, and you became
a woman chosen for motherhood;
not many to guide you or even explain
those aches in the heart not understood
by child or man, and are carried alone.
Who but the bearer knows the cost
of parting with something so singly blessed
as the fruit of first labour?   When the womb
and cradle share emptiness, love suffers most.

I see you now beyond that winter night,
when the farm, the cot, and death of a son
have faded again into candlelight.
The look in your eyes remains unchanged,
holding not one but a thousand years
of sorrow for all who have ever known
that proud dream of morning, when earth
promised more than the stars could show,
and hope sang like a lark in the girl's mouth.

THE PUMP

(for Ada and Douglas Cole)

You have made your water pump
into a garden ornament, painted it green
　　　and dressed it with geraniums
　　　to disguise what it had been
　　when this house was a farm on a tump
　　of grazing land between two languages.

Ours was a black iron brute
on guard outside our kitchen door, bidden to serve
　　　four other families.　It could
　　　heave water from its deep cave
　　in bucketfuls, splashing on our boots
　　small mercury beads of silent cadences.

Its trough shone with the green slime
of ages, reflecting always the gargoyle-grin
　　　of an uncouth mouth from which came
　　　monsters in my dreams;　each sin
　　a child committed was a dark crime
　　recorded by the furies in that well.

Our mothers told us the pump
had ears as old as ghosts.　Each limping clank
　　　of its long handle was the beat
　　　of a heart, and when we drank
　　of its water we could hear the thump
　　of time's blood knocking like a tolling bell.

11

I think of that narrow street
with its singular language, and of the sad
women toiling each day to fill
their buckets and pots. They had
no flowers to praise or make discreet
the wrinkles life brought early to each brow.

But it gave water, and I,
because of it, was fed, cleaned, healed, and so received
more than the secrets of a well,
more than what was later loved
for my smug self. Now, from this far, dry
nettles blossom, and these late petals grow.

THE SHED

The tiled roof of the shed had holes
through which, on winter nights, I could see stars
when I was made to help my father chop
the sticks we always needed for our fires.

'Kindling!' he'd say. 'It's time we chopped
some kindling. ' And so with axe and lamp we'd trek
the gravel-path to where the wood was kept;
the hovel, full of mice, was cold and dark.

He cleaved the logs, leaving the sticks
for me to fumble into dusty sacks.
Sometimes he'd struggle with a stubborn knot
gnarled like a tumour deep inside the bark.

Then I'd explore the slanting roof
hoping that through a hole I'd find a star
flashing its light to warn me from the rocks
on which I might have grounded in my fear.

It was my secret world, a fire
that touched the unlit tinders in my blood.
One day, I thought, these tiles will not be here
and I shall see a million stars instead.

'Wake up!' my father said, shoving
another pile of kindling at my feet.
The lamp was fading as I filled the sack,
my fingers cold with splinters of frost-bite.

Back in the warm and gas-lit house
my star was now much farther from the earth
as I sat staring at the teasing flames
making strange patterns flit across the hearth.

Today that shed is just a space
in someone else's garden, its old bricks
buried under beds of flowers, our rooms
now shadows drowned in seas of grass. What breaks

the memory never can rebuild
those walls, the logs, the roof of broken tiles.
The axe has lost its edge and empty hands
ache more with what the cold of silence tells.

YELLOW FLAG-IRISES

They were all I could give,
wildflowers stolen from the riverside
one summer morning when a boy
desperately needed to express
that most difficult of feelings – love.

All I could think of was that you,
my always-there, busy-about-the-house
mother, were ill in bed, and I,
not knowing whether you would
ever get well again, wanted to say

a lifetime of 'sorrys', as if
there'd not be time to make amends
for all the ways I'd wounded you
with crueller words
that children can be guilty of.

Nor, as a child of ten,
could I describe exactly how I felt
for someone who had spared
nothing of herself.   Those flowers
were my only feelings then.

I put them in a jar
hoping their colours would perform
a miracle. They were, I said, a gift
from nature.   It was too late
when I could offer more in summers after.

FORBIDDEN FLOWERS

'Don't pick the poppies or you'll wet the bed.'
I looked to see if you were serious
then knew I must not add those tempting flowers
to ones already wilting in my hand.

That such brash beauty was forbidden
was something I could never understand.
They beckoned to be touched, plucked
from the summer grass to take back home

to give our house the colour that it lacked.
I did not know, nor could I then believe
they'd make a child incontinent at night;
I still desired their petals of bright silk.

But I was forced to leave them where they were
because to touch them would make me ashamed.
I saw each scarlet rash of poppies then appear
as undesirable as measles or bad dreams.

Much later, when I'd grown, I stole
those fragile bits of summer from the fields
and learned, like any beauty which we are denied,
they had not lost their power to beguile.

FOLDINGS

Our two hands had not touched like that
since fifty years ago I helped her fold
the white sheets from the washing-line.
Starting apart we shook each one
from head to foot, from left to right,
until it shortened and our hands
met like the hands of those who meet
in stately order at a dance.

You take your end, I'll take mine.
Fold and double-fold, don't let go.
It was a ritual that made
each Monday-morning Reckett's-blue
and taught me innocently of love.
Now she lies white with hands that will
not tug or pull at sheets again,
or shorten longer distances.

With her late death a childhood dies
and there's no point in asking questions now.
Nor can my words begin to tell
the double grief I feel.   The path
where once we stood and laughed
is gone; but somewhere I still hear –
You take your end, I'll take mine.
Fold and double-fold, don't let go.

THE PIANO

Somewhere behind the fret-worked front
and two brass candlesticks was a sound
my father said was there but I could never find.

He'd bought the old piano at a sale
(together with a sideboard) for a pound,
its keys already yellow as a horse's teeth.

He had this fixed conviction in his mind
that if I practised several hours a day
I would become another Rubinstein.

'We've always had musicians in our family',
he'd say, though most achieved no more
than playing something in the town's brass band.

But every day, while all my friends
went off to fish or fly their kites,
I'd sit at that piano, fingers stretched,

trying to find the music still entrapped
behind that iron-frame and fading fret.
There was no sign of Bach or Chopin yet.

Then one year, half-way through the war,
a soldier came on Sunday nights to share
our meal and, afterwards, seduce those keys

from which I'd picked but boring scales.
I saw my father gloating in his pride
as this Welsh stranger proved for all to see

there was great music deep inside
the instrument I hated now so bitterly.
My ears grew deaf to every tune and trill.

What did it matter that the stuff he played
was by Ketèlbey, or variations
on some now forgotten masterpiece?

He made those ivories sing whilst I
grew smaller at his envied skills
and went to bed sick at the thought of him.

Whatever dreams my father had for me
died when that soldier left the town.
The battle then with Chopin was my own.

Years later, sitting at someone's
Steinway to admire its looks, I found
beneath my trembling hands those sounds

that had eluded me. My fingers touched
a chord that suddenly released
the notes of Mozart, Schubert, Liszt.

By then I knew those keys would not express
what now I felt I had to say.
I closed the lid, locked the regrets away

and wrote this coda with a silent pen.
The music that my father heard is still
as distant as my words are now to him.

THE WIRELESS AERIAL

(for David Twigg)

Twice as high as the clothes-line,
it went from pole to pole like rigging
over the deck of our garden.

Because of it we could hear people
speaking in London and Big Ben tolling
silence for the evening news.

There wasn't much that aerial couldn't do –
music, plays and comedians filled up the house
like favourite relatives.

How words which were invisible
came through the air to drop the world
right on our doorstep puzzled me.

But pole to pole was nearer to the truth
than we perceived. One Sunday morning
came the thin dry voice of Neville Chamberlain.

We sat in autumn stillness round the room
as mourners waiting for a funeral.
I felt our aerial had let us down.

Yet what I now remember most
is not the war, the sirens, or the bombs,
but how a blackbird always sang

from the tall and rough-hewn mast
high as our roof, its notes vibrating
in a clear blue glass of sky.

He and the blossom on the garden wall
became a well of indescribable delight
from which those echoes now return.

And nothing can destroy that world
though words remain as difficult to find
as wavelengths lost among the stars.

INCIDENTAL MUSIC

Stranger things no doubt have happened
but not in our street, where men came home
from working in the brickyards and sat down
to suppers of boiled bacon and coarse bread.

My father switched on the wireless and said
'A new play starts tonight which will, it says,
enrage some listeners and upset the Church.'
We were not used to programmes meant to shock,

so what banned words would actors soon unlock?
I stood there washing by a bright coal fire,
my hands deep in the bowl, anxious to see
if we'd turn off the play before its end.

The Man Born to be King: How could that offend?
Then suddenly our room was filled with light
that changed our simple lives into a world
of sensuous beauty. Each phrase

cast its own spell until I was half-crazed
with wonder at the sounds which made
me deaf to words. Aroused, each week
I waited for those shock-waves of Ravel

more than the play.   Nothing could equal
that luminescent joy.   Into our house
not only Palestine but France and Spain
came like a bowl of wine – flute, strings and harp

bidding fresh dreams beyond all hope.
And I can never hear that music now
without I see that room and learn to know
how long it takes some buried words to grow.

22

BRICKYARD WORKERS
AT DAYBREAK

It was a sound between sleep
and being awake, like the first
stirring of birds when dawn breaks
and, for a child, it is still dark.

Down the length of the street
men were preparing for work,
strapping dockey-bags to their bikes,
checking their lamps.

Our neighbours always spoke
in muffled talk, their voices
rising and falling and fading away
like the tide going out.

Then, like migratory birds,
they took off for the kilns
where fire and clay, both night and day,
went on slowing making bricks.

Above the town brown wakes of smoke
curdled the turning sky,
and fifty cloud-high chimneys
caged-in the struggling light.

So we returned to sleep
if only to forget that we
one day would rise like them
and shiver in the dark.

BUTTER-FINGERS

I do not know why that word made him laugh
for he was hardly in light-hearted mood,
laid-off from work and ill all week in bed;
and I was not precocious then at five.

Nor am I sure why I was lying there
beside my father in that upstairs room,
unless I too was sick or put with him
so he had company rather than stare

at the cracked ceiling or rose-papered wall.
Yet we were not alone for on that date
our house received its first electric light
which was, I thought, some form of miracle.

'Just think,' my father said, 'from now on we'll
have daylight at the touching of a switch;
no more smoking oil-lamps or candlewicks.'
I sat like one made speechless by a spell.

The workman fixed the cable with small clips
on to the chimney-breast, but when he dropped
them on the floor my shyness snapped.
I shouted *Butter-fingers!* – trying perhaps

to make it sound like a forbidden word;
and father laughed, not that I'd found my tongue
but more, I feel, because I'd given wing
to his frustrations, lying there in bed,

when what he wanted most was to get up
and go back to his work of making bricks
rather than watching me and one more week
slip through his nervous, clumsy finger-tips.

FATHER'S WEDDING-RING

Too ornate for my taste,
the belt-and-buckle pattern
just a bit too brash
even for sentiment to overlook.
And so for twenty years
it's been kept in a box
of pins and paper-clips
with old, unposted stamps.

But looking at it now
I find small flecks of clay
from when his hands made bricks,
grey specks of harder days
when this bright ring of gold
was crusted with his sweat.
For sixty years it was
a witness to his faithfulness.

Yet still I could not wear it
whatever its design, or take
upon myself such singleness of mind.
It's not the ring I find too big
for, though bone of his bone,
I am the one that will not fit,
so put his last gift down
lest it should turn to stone.

DEATH OF AN UNCLE

(for Jack Alster)

The Marconi of the brickyards,
a radio-ham who spent his hours
between work-shifts probing
the wavelengths of the world,

lay there that morning like
a burnt-out valve, his ears
and nostrils plugged with cotton-wool,
his eyes forever fixed on distant stars.

Death was more honourable
and private then. The body
kept and guarded in the house
by loved-ones or the next-of-kin.

But I remember him all headphones
knobs and frequencies,
tracking an earthquake in Japan
or cries for help from sad Hungarians

terrorised by Russian tanks.
He was a genius at picking up
assassinations and rebellions
before the BBC got wind of them –

a gifted medium at a séance
calling dry voices from the air.
We all grew tense with expectation
as he repeated, 'Are you there?'

But when one night the world called him
he did not reply. The static
crackled in deaf ears, the stars
were frozen in his eyes.

FAILING SIGHT

Unable to find my reading-glasses
I am reminded of my great-aunt Emily
who, in her eighties, could still read
her King James bible with the naked eye,
its double-column print more clear to her
than I could see with words twice magnified.

I saw her sewing once by candlelight,
each stitch a measured hyphen of black thread,
the needle skimming swiftly through the hem
like stones on water playing 'ducks and drakes'.
She said she did not care for winter nights –
her ageing sight no longer what it was.

Now through the flickering dark I see that room –
between the shadows are two china-dogs,
a hand-embroidered text upon the wall,
and tassels hanging from the table-cloth
on which her ghost-like candle haunts,
and she a fortune-teller reading her own hands.

She mumbled words as vague as auguries –
'The day will come when lights will ruin eyes
and constant noise will turn the ears to stone'.
I look out from my window at the sky
clouded with poison from the earth
and doubt if even she would find the stars.

WHITER THAN THE SNOW

They told her it was time to take a bath,
but with her vacant smile she said –
    'I only ever bath on Saturday.'

This wasn't true as we all knew
for seventy years she bathed six nights a week,
    trying to be whiter than the snow.

But recently, and sadly, she's gone back
to days when as a child she washed
    in a zinc bath before the kitchen fire.

Those winter nights were cold, the stars
splintered with frost. Yet she scrubbed on
    keeping her body whiter than the snow.

'If cleanliness is next to godliness', she'd say,
'I'll teach the soap and water how to pray,
    let every bath-night wash my sins away.'

That's how religion soaked her to the bone
and why she sang *Wash me in the blood of the Lamb*
    and I shall be whiter than the snow.

But soon the water cooled, the fire went out,
her prayers held little comfort in the dark;
    and love became an ember in her grate.

Go easy with her, nurse, and let her take
a bath in her own time, for all she wants to be
    is whiter, whiter than the snow.

NEW YEAR'S EVE – 1997

(In memory of a brother who died 5.12.97.)

It was more than an old year
    giving way to the new;
such boundaries are questionable.
    Yet we still need
those moments to divide the days
    left empty now by friends
for whom raised glasses did not bring
    the lusty greetings
of a midnight bell.   This year
    the silence picked on you.

You never were the rowdy reveller
    but preferred to see
the waiting hand slide imperceptibly
    across the hour,
more like a move you'd make in chess;
    not that you valued
any less another year brought in
    without indulgences.
Your death out-played mortality
    and kept our game in check.

As boys we were as strangers
    in the same small house,
sharing a room, a bed, and all those fears
    that childhood knows.
Yet we were different.   I fought
    against submission
whilst you surrendered calmly to become
    a shadow on the wall
until all wrath was spent.   I saw in you
    the Quaker then unborn.

It was through distances that we
    grew close, after
we'd left that long confining street
    to go beyond
the place where love was something more
    than we had understood.
It gave us freedom to become the friends
    our blood-ties made complete.
That was the gift your dying made us lose
    when wisdom came too late.

So as the midnight bell rang out
    its hammer blows
upon the changing year, I felt again
    the emptiness that comes
each time we raise those glasses
    which cannot be refilled.
Between our revelries a shadow passed
    that left a sudden chill,
like someone creeping quietly out of bed
    before the night is through.

TRACING MY FINGER NOW ON SIDEBOARD, CHAIRS

I can understand why for you each day
was only yesterday repeating itself –
getting up, clearing the ashes from the grate,
then polishing the hearthside brasses
before frost-leaves had faded from the window-panes.
Winter, no more than summer, did not complicate
your life but merely added to its drudgeries
like dust on furniture that would not go away.

You made the poker, tongs and fender shine
as if forged from the sun, then lit a fire
to bring the new day's comfort to a room
where we took warmth for granted, like our daily bread.
Such habit, duty, love but underlined
the safety of a home.   When we came
down the stairs each morning from our beds
we knew for certain what we'd always find.

But one by one your children did not sit
at places you had set; their absences
became those days your life would not repeat.
The dust was settling elsewhere and the hearths unswept.
I trace my finger now on sideboard, chairs, and bite
my lips to hide the loss another death completes.
I understand why you so often wept
in silence, trying to hold each unknown daybreak back.

THE DESTROYER

Those silver leaves upon the window-panes
are not as common now though frost still forms
slow-motion icicles along our eaves.

Outside, the cold is as it always was.
The water in the bird-bath hard as quartz,
the garden bushes looking grey and old.

Inside, our rooms are warm, so when we wake
we clear the misted glass and then admire
the frozen branches with their static blooms.

But still I see in memory that house
which had no heating in the rooms upstairs
and every pane had its own winter tree.

And I recall the wonder I then felt
that art should find its way into our world
where all we had was cheap and practical.

For those few days such intricate designs
intrigued me, brought creation close
to my small finger-tips, where ice amazed.

But too afraid to live with beauty long
I wilfully erased each silver leaf
by breathing on the glass and so betrayed

the gift I had received. That was not all.
I let the satisfaction cloud my mind
and learned too late how childhood had deceived.

CARROTS

Scraping the carrots today unearthed a smell
of sixty years ago when we, as boys,
were made to dig the school allotments
which once had been the Workhouse grounds
where paupers earned their parish bread.

The ruins of those buildings were still there,
the dead rooms haunted by their plaintive sounds.
Some days the shadows stretched across
the rows of vegetables we'd learned to grow
as part of our brief education's fare.

'Now bend your backs,' the teacher said,
'and use your forks to loosen round the roots,
then lift the carrots gently from the soil;
there is an art in gardening and more
to digging than you'll ever know.'

We did as we were told and shook the earth
from each bright bunch, breaking the best ones
from the stems to taste the smell
our morning lesson had released, more sweet
than any fruit the summer helped to swell.

Few now remember where the Workhouse stood,
no paupers limp down Drybread Road,
and I've forgotten most of what I learned
except that shadows seldom go away,
and some roots never leave the ground.

COME-UPPANCE

Scab-kneed and trailing a shoe-lace,
his toe-caps scuffed from kicking stones,
he prowled the street, wondering where next
his deeds could perpetrate some crime,
making old women curse him with clenched fists
or threaten him with 'calling the police'.

Skew-capped, with socks down to his ankles,
he eyed each window-pane and door,
each line of washing which would fall
if he knocked down the clothes-prop, or
which poor neighbour he could tease
by mimicking his limp or trembling jaw.

Fox-eyed with cunning and so quick
no one could out-manoeuvre him,
he was a devil out of evil bred,
a street-wise bully, full of cheek
who showed no fear because he'd proved
it paid to make the other side feel sick.

Cock-sure and daring in design
he climbed the church's spire to remove
the weather-vane.   But when the clock
struck three it filled his soul with dread
and down he dropped unpegged from grace,
a fallen garment from God's washing-line.

THAT PLACE, THOSE HOURS

(In Memoriam – F.R.)

I did not think to write an elegy for you –
a friend whom I'd not seen for forty years,
until a boy passed by with sun-burnt skin
and from the sky a lark spilt notes of rain.

Then I remembered one hot summer day
when we played cricket in long meadow grass,
where cows stood watching every eager run
you notched in chalk upon your mellow blade.

I bowled for hours, shirt off, and unaware
of how the heat was blistering my back,
whilst you hit out, reluctant to declare
until you'd equalled Bradman's highest knock.

Then when my innings came I had the luck
to be distracted by a lark that rose
as your late-swinger hit my middle stump.
I claimed "no ball" but you'd hear none of that.

The hurt was worse than any peeling skin
and lasted for a month, or maybe more.
And so we parted company, still friends,
but never to recall our epic match.

Now houses crouch like fielders in the slips,
the grass is gone and there's no room to bat;
and you, I hear, at sixty have been caught
whilst I, amazingly, am still not out.

That place, those hours, the summer I thought lost,
were all brought back because a boy passed by
stripped to the waist and, from a heap of stones,
a new bird rose to haunt an empty sky.

A CHANGE IN THE CLIMATE

One day the waters will force us back
to where we belong, to the estranged hills
and abandoned farms that our forefathers
were driven from by a landlord's greed.

But our songs will not be of returning,
nor of those sorrows in a place where blood
darkened the soil when men were manacled
to a land fashioned out of an old flood.

We shall sing first of those skies that loomed
over our harvests, remembering neighbours
who, for five generations, made art
out of fields through the pains of their labour.

We shall think too of the fear in their hunger
and of those women who bore their children
to rise from despair and one fine morning
walk through the gates of an open border.

When the sea refuses the rivers, when dykes
no longer contain the waters that pour down
from high country, we shall lock our doors
for the last time and trek back to old hearthstones,

some to the west, others to the north, each
obeying those routes when the blood recalls
where the first couples met, where the hills promised
something their love thought was paradise.

And then we shall sing because, for their sakes,
we will have finished the journey.   It will not be
the fire or sword but the returning waters
that will end our exile and bring us home.

THE INHERITOR

He will go on ploughing
even when his fields are no longer there,
    when the last furrow
has been turned and buried under the weight
    of a greedy city,
and the sun admits it has given up earth
    like a lost child.

But he who year after year
fashioned the clods of his land to bear fruit
    (counting them like sheep
as he went to sleep on his dying farm),
    will turn over the shares
even when the day's light no longer shines
    on the coulters' steel.

It will not be because
he has failed in his skills or love of the soil,
    but because nature
(that quirky mistress with an ace up her sleeve),
    will have decided
that he has held the tenancy long enough,
    so the deal is up.

Reclaimed from water
the fields will return either to swamp or go
    down under concrete,
fertile only for noise and the brash substitutes
    that a soul needs –
faith in the neon-lights and pleasures that pall
    when a heart dies.

He is not a man to shed tears,
yet I know the sorrow he will feel when days
        are not as he wished,
riding over the acres of a world that was
        not only his breath
but the land that his father and fathers had farmed
        and is no longer his.

ASKING AGAIN

You have kept me this side
of the day's darkness before,
now I beg you again to
surrender part of your sleep
to keep me from falling
into uncertain night
where fear stares like
a surgeon's knife into each
crevice of my mind.

Only you know how to forgive,
to heal one who has fled
like a wilful child
through the forbidden rooms
of a strange house.
Where should I be?   What
should my head be saying now
to justify another chance
of coming home?

I count my deaths beyond
the fingers of one hand, knowing
there must be reason
for each late reprieve. But this?
This shadow on the door
is all too real. So I will ask,
'Keep me from falling earthwards
that some task may be wrought
to pay old debts.'

SUNDAY AFTERNOON
IN A FENLAND CEMETERY

The lonely bring their flowers
to put in vases that seldom leave
the one place where the departed
feel forever safe. They walk
in ones or twos on gravel paths
between the graves laid out
like city squares; widows mostly,
or those grieving for children
who did not live beyond their love.

A February sun softens
the whiteness of memorial stones
and warms the bronze chrysanthemums
which awkward hands arrange
as if to prolong a ritual
for which the purpose is not clear.
They know only week by week
the dead must be remembered
however old and stripped their bones.

This part of town already has
a feeling of eternity. When voices speak
they have a distance and solemnity
that turns them into living ghosts.
One woman hugs a watering-can
as if it were a man held in her arms;
another kneels and utters words
the years or weathers will not fade
until the last bright morning breaks.

Yet that may never be, for soon
these graves may all be drowned
as earth surrenders to the rising sea,
each granite cross and tomb
submerged beneath the flood
like sunken boats upon an ocean bed;
their epitaphs and memories washed away
as nature claims again the land
it lost to make this burial-ground.

How then shall we respect the dead
hidden by water from the sun,
or place our footsteps on those paths
along which mourners now return?
Better those ashes that were blown
over an untamed fen, where words
were given to the wind, and grief
unheard.   There are some deaths
for which no flowers can atone.

But still I find it hard to leave
before they lock the gate
for there are those of my own kin
lying beneath this green –
four generations and my father's son
who died before my life began.
And how shall I remember them
with something worthier than tears
or the cold wreaths of regret?

A CHANGE OF VIEW

I am beginning to wish we had mountains,
not to ascend or to breed premature shadows
from the sun, but to serve as a measuring-stick
as only rocks can.   It is not that I ask
for a beauty beyond that which we have,
nor desire to block the generosity of light
on a land that has given more height to the heart
than any peak my lowland feet might climb.
But how does a man gauge his years unless
some image be projected on the face
of prehistoric lava petrified?

All earth is ancient, fused out of the same
chemistry that forged the deserts, forests, ice.
Is not water as old as stone?   Does not mist
possess a history as durable as rock?   But
can we trust the vacillating needle on a stream
or weigh the worth of each capricious cloud?
We need sometimes the more substantial things
to check our watches by, to cut us down to size.
As well as distance we require great hills
to stand against, a frequent change of view
for faith and longing to be satisfied.

AND WHAT IS SUMMER STILL

Summer, in more than name,
Days of slow motion in a curve of light;
the sound of children's games
in neighbouring gardens; the click of bat
on ball; the unclaimed time
where nothing need disturb the afternoon.

But there are notes beyond
the ones of this last brooding season
that tremble in the mind;
memories of long neglected gardens
where shadows till the ground;
these are the summers that we lose too soon.

And further off the drift
of voices, soft as petals that always fall
from lack of rain, the weft
of those deep moments which return to spoil
our idleness; the puffed
dandelion-clock; the flowers that now wound.

Then through the heat-haze comes
the scent of meadows and a shaded house
doused in geraniums;
the gentle conversation where thoughts pause
until the silence seems
more eloquent than any speech words found.

There, too, the narrow lane
of hawthorn-froth and poppy-stippled grass;
        a pond, an open barn,
and then a field of corn as bold as brass;
        and larks so near the sun
they are invisible in all but song.

        And what is summer still
without the woodwind cadences of doves,
        the secret dreams that steal
like heavy bees returning to dark hives?
        We take each year and feel
its ripeness, whether it was right or wrong.

        So certain days are pressed
like leaves that lose their colour and their smell
        until they're almost dust;
the sounds we hear belong, however small,
        to what we thought we'd lost
and, even in their sadness, make us whole.

FEELING EARTH PAUSE

The hour of long shadows over grass
    has its own stillness;
the sky, cloud-clear as glass, would
    if flicked by the wind's finger,
      ring as a fine goblet;
perfection perched on the stem of evening.

Somewhere between shadow and light
    a lark sings as though
his task was in the making of stars
    before earth slips like a spark
      from the sun's grasp,
leaving us only with a drained cup.

There are sounds other than those last notes
    of a bird that will itself
turn into a star.   Sheep with sore throats
    baa from the hills, their cries
      unchanged since Time began,
their language pitched always about one word.

And for a moment we, like the fields,
    hold our breath until
the shadows kneel down with the beasts,
    feeling earth pause on its axis
      as if it too needed
its own stillness to fold day within dark.

CAUGHT ON A MORNING

It is like birth, though waking into middle-age
    has benefits unknown to those
who for the first time meet the day's new light.

Eyes open, remembering that what they saw
    before they closed was endless dark;
night wrapped in its own swaddling clothes.

But as the lids unfurl, tall trees appear
    where shadows were and finger-tips
of sun reach for the pale, embarrassed trunks

of ash and sycamore, which then draw back
    as if too modest to be seen.
Yet hands, instinctively, know when to touch

and light is never static. It gently feels
    its way between each leaf and branch,
allowing earth to stretch itself awake.

Above the trees the sky, too, is unclothed
    except for one loose vapour-thread
caught on a morning that began elsewhere.

IN AN ALIEN HEAVEN

Suddenly, in the sea-blue sky, a lark sang,
and there were no longer stones at my feet
but grass that had given its dew to the heat
of the sun a lifetime ago, and nothing
can bring back the past with such swiftness of joy
as the song of that bird, nor will the boy
be forgotten though his days are diminishing.

Suddenly, there in an alien heaven,
where hills obscured the sky-line, a sound
so exquisite was heard from the pebbled ground
that I was granted a second chance even
to rise from the grass I had known as a child
and dance, as if all my years had been whiled
away in that place where the first joy was given.

HERON

Pond-robber,
parachuting in like a dawn-raider
camouflaged against grey sky,
as if a piece of cloud had dropped
to shadow the tense water
where fish freeze under
your cold and practised eye,
knowing your beak's karate chop
is one that will not falter.

Why do we praise you,
follow your flight over tree-top
and pasture, as if a god
from some mythology had come
to visit us? Talisman, without whom
no journey is complete,
we applaud your solitary silence,
pardon even the thief in you
for plundering our garden.

And now this print
we've framed to hang upon our wall
confirms your deity. See how your wings
spread like the holy ghost
over our lives, how grace is given
to immobility, how flight is more
than movement in fixed air.
You are the one now frozen in
a pool of light death cannot stir.

BIRDS IN MOURNING

Staring into the shallows of bright grass
we watch the shadows of the swallows' flight
weaving frail nets across the summer tide,
giving our noon-day images of night.

The birds are teaching fledglings how to swim
like fish through air inebriate and warm.
Above the fields their grace and skill amaze;
such swiftness on the wing defies all harm.

But soon a hawk with shark-like eyes swoops down
to snatch one new-born swimmer from the skies,
and on that troubled sea the nets unwind,
the pattern falls apart, a shadow dies.

Now birds in mourning make their sad cries wound
a world this day will never comprehend.

THE SUNFLOWER

With too many thoughts in its head
to stand upright, its thick neck bent
with the weight of a hangover
and all its energy spent,
the ageing sunflower cannot hide
a face too weary to recover
the bold appearance it once had
when it was young and arrogant.

With spine no longer sure or straight,
and leaves limp as a washing-cloth,
it leans against the garden fence
and slowly comes to terms with death.
The promise shown came all too late,
there seldom is a second chance;
now, one by one, the seeds falls out,
leaving the hollow head a wreath.

And what, when dying is achieved,
is left of all that summer gave?
Even the gaudiest petals fade,
years dim the furnaces of love.
Yet this one flower that has revolved
around the seasons of each mood,
has pressed its image, page by page,
on words that only love will prove.

WAR-CEMETERY – POLAND

There are several reasons for sunflowers.
In isolation they are like scarecrows
stranded in English gardens, their heads
lolling from side to side, with no sense
of where the next day's sun will rise.
They show a heavy weariness, as if
their thoughts outweighed the wish
to stand upright.   It is a poor disguise
which, clown-like, makes the owners smile
to see them lean half-drunk against the fence.

Others, more free to tantalise the wind,
sway in large fields and openly display
a furnace of bright gold – flames
twisting across the earth to praise
the joy of warmth and surge of summer light.
One day their seeds will ooze sweet oil
and wise uplifted heads still turn
to follow the sun's downfall into night.
Child-like, they'll see each timely death
as a brief darkness wedged between long days.

But I remember now another scene
where they grew solemnly on soldiers' graves,
sunflowers reaching for the great sun's rays
as if to give back life to those below;
each head benevolent with hope
for limbs that could not move. What saves
a man from his perpetual night
more than the promise of his soul's escape?
Erect, and for inspection dressed,
they stood unbowed, where wounds no longer show.

SURVIVOR

You are the pressed leaf in a book
when all the leaves of that dark season
are gone into the ground, or have blown
like smoke into the barbed air.

You have left your imprint on the page –
vein, shape and colour of a year
that out of desperation made you seek
another tongue with which to say

"this I will do for all who would have loved
had other arms than death's embraced their bones.
I take each burning moment as it comes
to celebrate the joy they could not find."

Few see the nervous shadows in a room
or watch the mirror image crack with tears.
A private world has other doors to lock;
your body trembles with six million fears.

And you are there between each word –
name, breath and witness to an age
earth struggles to disown.   A death
that will not die.   A tree reborn.

THE FACE
(on a self-portrait of Käthe Kollwitz)

for Lotte and Fritz Kramer

Look at the white hair of sorrow,
the eyes half-buried in shadow.
It is the face of a thousand years
of suffering, the face of all mothers
weeping for their lost children
and of all widows mourning
for husbands who disappeared
in wars, labour-camp or prison.

See how the lips are silent as stone,
her cheeks a mask failing to hide
that desperate need to be held
in the arms of someone who was proof
of the heart's power to survive,
even though evil plotted to destroy
all that was noble in her mind,
and darkness threatened the sun's light.

Look at the anguish in her face,
at the grief no tears can wash
from eyes that have no time for flowers
nor by apology will be appeased.
It is a face that has been there
wherever women wept, speaking
of all those deaths nursed in the breast
of every Niobe, Antigone and Ruth.

And there are those whose sorrows
are not yet, whose loss will not
be played upon some stage but fill
a once-shared room with emptiness.
She wears their silence too, knowing
how heavy is the shadow of a cross
that will not let the memory sleep,
though love itself is sealed in rock.

YOU ASK ME WHAT
I'M GOING TO PUT ON

I was going to wear black
but I have mourned long enough
and wearing black will not make any difference now.

Beyond the drum-beat,
beyond the muffled tolling of a bell,
there must be something more to ease our suffering.

I do not mean those griefs
that in some measure we articulate
when someone dies who cannot be replaced,

but those cold tears each age
will shed upon a generation's grave
because the best of all that was, withered like flowers.

Too many mourners weep
over the ashes of a world
heavy with tombstones, elegies and uneasy guilts.

True, there are some deaths
we ought to stand in silence for,
wearing our solemn masks to hide the looks of shame –

I think of all those victims
of unpardonable wars, who fell
because deep hatred bred new passions for a worn-out creed.

So who corrupted love,
computerised a lie to make it truth?
And who deprived the unborn of their innocence?

We have so many blames to bear,
so many reasons why we now believe
each twilight breeds its own dread of eternity.

Yet, is there not still time
for one new day to ride in on the sun
giving us one more chance to dance, to sing?

I watch the dawn emerge
with huge relief out of some nightmare.
And when you ask me what I'm going to put on, I'll say:

I was going to wear black
because I am familiar with earth's ritual.
But wearing black will not make any difference now.

So I'll put on my gold-braid
tunic and peaked-cap then wake the town
with resurrection blasts upon my Gabriel trumpet.

EVENING LIGHT

Edward Hopper would have caught
    this moment accurately –
two people in a room
    now separated by a continent.

Outside, the evening light
    gives trees some certainty
before their shadows merge
    with those that night makes permanent.

And silently the man and woman fade
    into their wordless dark,
hoping that love will survive –
    a miracle, a work of art.

LOST DAYS

It is the distance that brings you close,
as though a river over-flowed
and lapped its waters at this house
which several counties separate
from the familiar boundaries.

There's no horizon here.   The sky
is now a frieze for city roofs
that block out light.   Walls tremble
at the winds cry, squinting an eye
at the wild swans' incredible flight.

I can feel tonight your warm hands
touching again that ageing nerve
caught in the rib's claw, knowing
I should have stayed where there's no need
to ask who is the betrayer, or betrayed.

But there is balm in this recurring thought –
that you will never let me down
or fail in your forgiving that old flaw
found in the blood, or turn away
from a man begging in uncaring streets.

END OF TERM

They are gathering in rows upon the grass,
each class now posing for its photograph;
children assembled neatly into years
they'll never see again.   Some laugh,
some try a permanent smile, all
caught for this last moment in an age
that will remind them of a day that was.

They know today their school is breaking up
for summer holidays but not, when they return,
how they'll have changed – for nothing stays
as timeless as the grins they're offering
to the camera.   Soon they will learn
to smile in far more subtle ways,
for innocence, like childhood, does not keep.

So watching them this morning I can see
beyond the undeveloped film what each
child will become some twenty years away –
stressed-out and wondering how to cope
with their own offspring for so many weeks.
Will they then take this print of former days
to search in vain for something yet to be?

The classes now disperse and, one by one,
the boys and girls rejoicingly go home,
leaving not emptiness where laughter was
but ageless ghosts upon the uncut grass.
Each year I see a generation last
for three brief terms before the shutters close.
And always something more than age is lost.

A GIRL WRITING

(after the painting by Sophie Bouteiller Descaux)

Where should the eye first rest, on child or bird
or slim pen waiting for the timid word?

She sits, distracted from her morning task,
her mind shaping each question she would ask.

A bird, freed for an hour from its cage,
is perched near her elbow.   But on the page

the words are not so easy to release.
Her apples, books, ink and the next line, cease

to exist until replies are found.
'How do you sing so naturally, your sound

filling my room whilst, even though I try,
my pen stays dumb and words refuse to fly?

'How came your gift of song with such great ease
whilst mine is full of dark uncertainties?'

He has no answers she will understand.
The dry-nibbed pen stays in her gentle hand

as if it were an arrow caught in flight.
The bird looks up.   For him there's no delight

in singing when he is not free.   True song
belongs upon the bough.   He deems it wrong

that talent should be locked within bare walls.
It is through air each perfect cadence falls.

The thoughtful child sees then how it will be
when she is caught by age, or flattery.

MONUMENTS

The leaf just fallen from my book
once hung over Beethoven
brooding on his pedestal
in a wreath of plane trees.

It is the same green that his cloak
would have been, threadbare,
the veins prominent as seams
holding together something that's hardly there.

I think of those trees shedding bark
to protect themselves from the dirt
we spawn in our cities, pollution
strangling what still needs to breathe –

music, art, the uncorrupted word,
and all that is dying – first the leaves,
then the trees, then the bare earth
which will be our monument.

BEETHOVEN'S STATUE

It is right that you are brooding alone
under the dying trees of a noisy Vienna,
set apart from the place where every path
has its own monument; isolated
in the depths of unfathomable torment.

The bronze is your deafness – heavy,
silent, impenetrable.   No thunder
can break now through the shell of your ear;
the sculptor has preserved what he found
in the dark chamber of your mind.

Not even the gods at your feet can rise
to a brow still pensive with the weight
of your questioning.   It is not anger
so much as the sorrow of one
pondering on why a man should receive

the divine gift of fire yet be denied
its benevolence, being bowed down
with the Promethean chains of silence
in a world without sound
until freed from the grip of earth's last rock.

BEETHOVEN

First the furnace of the sun
deep in the skull; the cells of your brain
burning with the beginnings of a world
as yet unborn.
What order will break from such chaos of fire
is still to be seen.   Only your skill
will match each miracle
or shackle the elements your moods require
to fill the firmament with stars.

Now out of silence, out of sleep,
out of that mysterious hour, your blood
leaps with a joy unleashed as light
floods through your head.
Planets and galaxies explode in the dark
as your fingers touch the boundaries
of space.   You are earth's god
wrestling with Titan for that hidden power
needed to make creation work.

Before mountains were brought forth
or ever the earth and the world were made,
you were at the heart of its making,
waiting to breathe,
to give birth, to re-order our genesis, to
open the eyes of a race that was blind,
slanting the rays of the sun
towards the darkness of our land, breaking
even the stones into flowers.

And so the whole universe
was gathered into your mind to be released –
your ears defying their prison bars,
hearing music
beyond what deafness might deny or death out-last.
Towering above mountains and vast seas
your only equal was the sky
where other worlds of suns, moons, stars, await
the moment you will set them free.

SCHUBERT

And you, Franz!   Forgive the familiarity
but you are one of those unmet friends
whose warmth transcends the formality
of shaking hands; affection which depends
on physical awareness eventually
declines.   Love is the touching of two minds.

So we approach you, sitting now alone
in Vienna's shade, not overshadowed
any more by one who keeps his own
thoughts on a bronze pedestal, hallowed
always as he was by you.   To be made one
with him is a gift Time has bestowed.

And we embrace you too because you knew
beneath the sunlight on clear streams crept
shadows which, when darkness came, grew
monstrous in the night.   Most joys have slept
with sorrow, but even when tears fell you
gave us music although the tired earth wept.

GOOD FRIDAY – SPAIN

It could have been here
where creation ran out of ideas,
that the shaped tree was dragged
through the shouting crowds
for a man to prove how faith
can survive even a pierced side.

There is little to show now
in the stones and ungathered thorns
how death was prolonged one afternoon
so that a town could celebrate
with fireworks and trumpets
its liberation from the threat of love.

But listen, and in the April wind
you'll hear his timeless words
haunting this wilderness – *Father,*
forgive.   And from the one tree
not yet demolished by developers,
blossoms a flower, red as blood.

THE BEES OF ST GUTHLAC

The polyphony of bees' chant
in a cloister of lupins
lifts thought beyond boundaries
to a place where I hear
the bees of an older order
conducting their liturgies
in the walls of an abbey
laid bare for centuries.

Each year for my ritual
I stand near those crevices
to share in the dark buzz of prayer
droning from stones scarred
by fire and sword when greed
shattered love's sanctuary,
leaving the earth blood-stained
and deprived of its flowers.

And before the bees was a man
who sat in his cloisters
telling birds where to build,
offering water from his cup
to any lame or untamed animal.
Everything touched by his hand
grew, or was healed. His mind knew
more than the wisdom of seasons.

If anyone came to his door
they too would find shelter,
receiving both honey and wine
from his stone jar.   Sometimes
I feel he is still there,
giving answers to questions
we cannot find speech for,
drawing deep from his mind's well.

The bees in this borrowed garden
remind me again of how much
we need to share silence,
to go where the stones reply.
I listen and hear more than the power
of wings probing a flower;
I feel the breath on my face
of peace I have known elsewhere.

SOMETHING OF A GAMBLE

The wet sycamore seeds lie on the path
like large tadpoles in a drained pool,
their evolution ended by a heartless wind.

Unsentimental nature does not ease
the autumn out with courtesy or grace
but wrecks destruction through its ageing trees.

Some seeds might slither inch by inch
to hibernate in grass and there take root
to spawn another generation in the spring.

Then we, with rake, fork, spade or trowel,
will pull them out to join the pile of weeds
that have no chance to flourish in the sun.

The odds are all too great, the going rough.
So many promises have died because
the climate changed.   It is the same with us.

AN OLD POET READING
TO A YOUNG AUDIENCE

Even when they looked up
they saw no more than a shadow,
someone in period costume
stepping wearily out of a book,
or walking back into a museum
where the dying as well as the dead go
when there's no one to listen.

I watched them politely
applauding the old man's song,
not for what he had sung
but because the singing was done –
his voice parchment, his words
dry on the tongue. They had forgotten
that once he was young.

When he walked from the hall,
his eyes hollow, his hair
white as the marble of a Roman tomb,
only one girl stared at the door,
aware of how some presences can chill.
The rest waited, as always,
for the beat of a new drum.

THE UNWANTED SOLITUDE

Glimpsed between dark and light,
caught by the lava eye of death's camera,
who would believe the gaping mouth
with terror in its throat was once
a laughing boy, a man who let
the heart express love's plenitude?

Frozen in stone, those lips
encircle not a song but the unfinished scream
of one for whom the night had been
a dream of stars enhancing sleep,
filling his proud and youthful ears
with earth's applauding multitude.

How many times must love
die in the nightmare-nakedness of truth,
breaking its seventh wave upon
grey rocks? Earthquake and fire remove
the joy of consummation to debase
the body's unspoilt pulchritude.

Now he lies petrified
in the volcanic ashes of lust's grip.
What else is death but the last act
of nature to destroy, to wreck all hope
bred in the womb and for birth's promise give
the grave's unwanted solitude.

EXPERIENCE

I am only just beginning to find the answers
when it's almost too late to ask the questions.

It's like being told I can fly when my
wings have been clipped to make flight impossible.

I find it most inconsiderate of life
to be blessed with such wisdom in one's old age.

Imagine, all that learning gone up in smoke
before we pass through the gates of the crematorium.